Science and Nature

Uncover the mystery of everyday marvels, from rocks to rainbows

ENCYCLOPÆDIA
Britannica®

CHICAGO   LONDON   NEW DELHI   PARIS   SEOUL   SYDNEY   TAIPEI   TOKYO

PROJECT TEAM

Judith West, *Editorial Project Manager*
Christopher Eaton, *Editor and Educational Consultant*
Indu Ramchandani, *Project Editor (Encyclopædia Britannica India)*
Bhavana Nair, *Managing Editor (India)*
Rashi Jain, *Senior Editor (India)*
Kathryn Harper, *U.K. Editorial Consultant*
Colin Murphy, *Editor*
Locke Petersheim, *Editor*
Nancy Donohue Canfield, *Creative Director*
Megan Newton-Abrams, *Designer*
Amy Ning, *Illustrator*
Joseph Taylor, *Illustrator*
Karen Koblik, *Senior Photo Editor*
Paul Cranmer, *Retrieval Specialist and Indexer*
Barbara Whitney, *Copy Supervisor*
Laura R. Gabler, *Copy Editor*
Dennis Skord, *Copy Editor*
Marilyn L. Barton, *Senior Production Coordinator*

**ENCYCLOPÆDIA BRITANNICA
PROJECT SUPPORT TEAM**

EDITORIAL

Theodore Pappas, *Executive Editor*
Lisa Braucher, *Data Editor*
Robert Curley, *Senior Editor, Sciences*
Brian Duignan, *Senior Editor, Philosophy, Law*
Laura J. Kozitka, *Senior Editor, Art, World Culture*
Kathleen Kuiper, *Senior Editor, Music, Literature, World Culture*
Kenneth Pletcher, *Senior Editor, Geography*
Jeffrey Wallenfeldt, *Senior Editor, Geography, Social Sciences*
Anita Wolff, *Senior Editor, General Studies*
Charles Cegielski, *Associate Editor, Astronomy*
Mark Domke, *Associate Editor, Biology*
Michael Frassetto, *Associate Editor, Religion*
James Hennelly, *Associate Editor, Film, Sports*
William L. Hosch, *Associate Editor, Math, Technology*
Michael R. Hynes, *Associate Editor, Geography*
Michael I. Levy, *Associate Editor, Politics, Geography*
Tom Michael, *Associate Editor, Geography*
Sarah Forbes Orwig, *Associate Editor, Social Sciences*
Christine Sullivan, *Associate Editor, Sports, Pastimes*
Erin M. Loos, *Associate Editor, Human Biology*
Anne Eilis Healey, *Assistant Editor, Art, World Culture*

DESIGN

Steven N. Kapusta, *Designer*
Cate Nichols, *Designer*

ART

Kathy Nakamura, *Manager*
Kristine A. Strom, *Media Editor*

ILLUSTRATION

David Alexovich, *Manager*
Jerry A. Kraus, *Illustrator*

MEDIA ASSET MANAGEMENT

Jeannine Deubel, *Manager*
Kimberly L. Cleary, *Supervisor, Illustration Control*
Kurt Heintz, *Media Production Technician*
Quanah Humphreys, *Media Production Technician*

CARTOGRAPHY

Paul Breding, *Cartographer*

COPY

Sylvia Wallace, *Director*
Larry Kowalski, *Copy Editor*
Carol Gaines, *Typesetter*

INFORMATION MANAGEMENT/INDEXING

Carmen-Maria Hetrea, *Director*

EDITORIAL LIBRARY

Henry Bolzon, *Head Librarian*
Lars Mahinske, *Geography Curator*
Angela Brown, *Library Assistant*

EDITORIAL TECHNOLOGIES

Steven Bosco, *Director*
Gavin Chiu, *Software Engineer*
Bruce Walters, *Technical Support Coordinator*
Mark Wiechec, *Senior Systems Engineer*

COMPOSITION TECHNOLOGY

Mel Stagner, *Director*

MANUFACTURING

Dennis Flaherty, *Director*

INTERNATIONAL BUSINESS

Leah Mansoor, *Vice President, International Operations*
Isabella Saccà, *Director, International Business Development*

MARKETING

Patti Ginnis, *Senior Vice President, Sales and Marketing*
Jason Nitschke, *National Sales Manager, Retail Advertising and Syndication*
Michael Ross, *Consultant*

ENCYCLOPÆDIA BRITANNICA, INC.

Jacob E. Safra,
Chairman of the Board

Ilan Yeshua,
Chief Executive Officer

Jorge Cauz,
President

Dale H. Hoiberg,
Senior Vice President and Editor

Marsha Mackenzie,
Managing Editor and Director of Production

Science and Nature

What are tsunamis?
Why did the dinosaurs disappear? Why do some leaves turn red?
What woman won *two* Nobel Prizes in the sciences?

In *Science and Nature,* you'll discover answers to these questions and many more. Through pictures, articles, and fun facts, you'll learn about weather, meet fascinating scientists, and see how plants and animals can change over time.

To help you on your journey, we've provided the following guideposts in *Science and Nature*:

■ **Subject Tabs**—The colored box in the upper corner of each right-hand page will quickly tell you the article subject.

■ **Search Lights**—Try these mini-quizzes before and after you read the article and see how much—*and how quickly*—you can learn. You can even make this a game with a reading partner. (Answers are upside down at the bottom of one of the pages.)

■ **Did You Know?**—Check out these fun facts about the article subject. With these surprising "factoids," you can entertain your friends, impress your teachers, and amaze your parents.

■ **Picture Captions**—Read the captions that go with the photos. They provide useful information about the article subject.

■ **Vocabulary**—New or difficult words are in **bold type**. You'll find them explained in the Glossary at the end of the book.

■ **Learn More!**—Follow these pointers to related articles in the book. These articles are listed in the Table of Contents and appear on the Subject Tabs.

Britannica®
LEARNING LIBRARY

Have a great trip!

A fallen maple leaf shows its autumn colors.

Science and Nature

TABLE OF CONTENTS

Introduction 3

SOME ESSENTIALS

Atoms: Building Blocks of Matter. 6

Liquids, Solids, and Gases:

Same Stuff, Different Forms 8

Echoes: Sounds That See in the Dark 10

Energy: The Power of Life 12

Leaves: The Science of Their Changing Colors 14

PHENOMENA OF NATURE

Temperatures: Hot and Cold. 16

Dew: Diamond Drops of Water 18

Clouds: Floating Water. 20

Rainbows: Arcs of Color. 22

Thunder and Lightning: Nature's Fireworks 24

Cyclones and Tornadoes: Nature's Fury 26

Acid Rain: Killer Downpour 28

Waves: Movement on the Seas 30

Tsunamis: Waves of Destruction 32

GEOLOGY: Studying the Earth 34

Rocks and Minerals:

The Earth's Building Blocks. 36

Chalk: The Remains of Tiny Shells 38

Sand: The Nitty-Gritty 40

Diamonds:

The Hardest-Working Gemstones in the World . . . 42

Volcanoes: Mountains of Smoke and Fire. 44

Fossils: Ancient Life in Stone 46

Dinosaurs: Giants of the Past 48

Dinosaurs: A Mystery Disappearance. 50

Tyrannosaur: The Tyrant King. 52

Mammoths and Mastodons: Ancient Elephants 54

NATURE SCIENTISTS

Luther Burbank: Inventing New Plants 56

Marie Curie: Discovering a New Kind of Science. . . . 58

Charles Darwin: The Theory of Evolution 60

Glossary 63

Building Blocks
of Matter

Everything in the world is made up of molecules. Our bodies, our clothes, our houses, animals, plants, air, water, sky—everything. Molecules are so small, though, that we can't see them with our naked eyes.

But molecules aren't the smallest things. Molecules are made up of atoms, which are smaller still. Atoms are so small that it takes more than a billion atoms to fill the space taken up by one pea!

The word "atom" comes from the Greek word *atomos*, meaning "**indivisible**." But despite what their name suggests, atoms can indeed be divided into smaller pieces. Each atom has a **core** called a "nucleus." Around the nucleus swarm small **particles** called "electrons." The nucleus itself is made up of other small particles called "protons" and "neutrons." And these protons and neutrons are made up of even smaller things called "quarks." So, for now at least, quarks are among the smallest known things in the universe.

LEARN MORE! READ THESE ARTICLES...
ENERGY · LIQUIDS, SOLIDS, AND GASES · MARIE CURIE

DID YOU KNOW?
Quarks are so small that scientists have to make up new ways to describe them. They talk about the different "flavors" of quarks—not chocolate or pistachio but "up," "down," "charm," "strange," "top," and "bottom."

e

e

e

e

e

e

e

SEARCH LIGHT

True
or false?
Atoms are the
smallest things
of all.

Answer: FALSE. Atoms can be split into electrons, neutrons, and
protons, all of which are smaller than the atom itself. And quarks
are even smaller than those.

Same Stuff, Different Forms

Did you know that many of the things you may see or use every day—such as the water in a glass, the air in a football, and even the hard metal in a toy car—are **potential** shape-shifters?

The substances that these things are made of can have the form of a solid, a liquid, or a gas. The form they take depends mostly on their temperature. When water gets cold enough, it becomes a hard solid we call "ice." When it gets hot enough, it becomes a wispy gas we call "steam." Many other substances behave the same way when they are heated or cooled enough.

A solid holds its own size and shape without needing a container. If you pour water into an ice tray and freeze it, the water will keep the shape of the cube-shaped molds in the tray. You can think of the solid metal in a toy car as frozen too, but its melting temperature is much higher than the temperatures we live in. The person who made the car poured very hot liquid metal into a car-shaped mold and let it cool down and freeze.

A liquid does not hold its own shape. If you pour a measuring cup of water into a tall glass or a shallow bowl, it will take the shape of its container. But that water does keep its own size. It measures one cup. Everyday liquids such as milk, paint, and gasoline act this same way.

Gases do not keep their own shape or their own size. When air is pumped into a football, it takes the shape and size of the ball. As more air is pumped in, the ball gets harder but not much bigger. The air changes its size to fit the space inside the ball.

LEARN MORE!
READ THESE ARTICLES...
ENERGY • TEMPERATURES
VOLCANOES

Mark whether each item below describes a solid (S), a liquid (L), or a gas (G). Some may match more than one form.

- melts
- turns into a liquid
- keeps shape
- has no shape or size
- is frozen
- has no shape

DID YOU KNOW?

If you've ever smelled gas coming from a stove, you know it has an odd odor. But cooking gas has no odor. What you're smelling is another gas with an odor that's easy to notice. It's mixed with the cooking gas so that people know when there's a leak.

Answer: melts = S; turns into a liquid = S, G; keeps shape = S; has no shape or size = G; is frozen = S; has no shape = L, G

Sounds That See
in the Dark

"**H**el-l-o-o-o-o-o!"

A boy hears the echo coming from the hills.

"Echo, talk to me," he calls.

"...to me," repeats the echo. "...to me...to me...to me."

What is an echo? It's a sound you make that bounces back to you from hills or other surfaces. But how can a sound bounce? It's not a ball.

Actually, sound is a wave in the air. If you could see air the way you see water, you'd see the waves that sounds make. Sound waves bounce only if they hit something big and solid like the side of a hill or the walls of a cave.

What if nothing stops the sound waves? Then they just get smaller and smaller. Or they are absorbed by soft things such as carpets, draperies, or large pieces of furniture. That's why we don't usually hear echoes in the house.

DID YOU KNOW?
It is said that a duck's quack is the only sound that doesn't echo. If you happen to have a duck and a long hallway, you could test this theory yourself.

Did you know that echoes can help some animals "see" in the dark?

In pitch-dark caves bats fly easily, never bumping into anything and even catching tiny insects in the air. As they fly, they make tiny whistlelike sounds. These sounds bounce back to them. The direction of the echo and the time it takes for it to return tell the bats exactly where things are as they fly.

Human beings have learned to harness the power of echoes for navigation too. Submarines traveling underwater use **sonar** to bounce sounds off of solid objects so that they can tell where those objects are located—sort of like undersea bats!

LEARN MORE! READ THESE ARTICLES…
ENERGY · RAINBOWS · WAVES

SEARCH LIGHT

What animal uses sound to "see"?

Answer: Bats use echoes to tell what is around them in the dark. Dolphins do the same thing underwater.

The Power of Life

Without energy in our bodies, we wouldn't be able to do anything. We couldn't walk, talk, or even play. Energy is usable power. And all energy is related to some kind of motion.

All living things need energy, no matter what they do. Plants get their energy from sunlight. This energy is stored in different **chemicals** inside the plant. This whole process is called "photosynthesis."

Animals that eat plants take the energy stored in the plants. The energy is then stored in chemicals inside the animals as "food energy." The same happens when animals eat other animals.

Plants and animals use food energy every day as they grow and do the work of being a plant or an animal. So plants have to keep **absorbing** sunlight, and animals have to keep eating plants or other animals.

It isn't only living things that have energy. A dead tree has hidden energy. When we burn its wood, it gives off warmth, or "heat energy." The Sun too makes heat energy as it constantly burns.

The Sun gives off not just heat but also light, as "light energy." A battery in a flashlight makes it shine, **generating** light energy. But if we put the same battery in a radio, we get music. A battery's energy is known as "electrical energy." And in a toy car that electrical energy produces movement, or "kinetic energy."

If we couldn't use heat, light, or electrical energy, we couldn't drive cars or cook food. We wouldn't have light at nighttime. Basically, we'd have to use the energy of our own bodies. And that would mean eating a lot more and doing a lot less.

LEARN MORE! READ THESE ARTICLES…
MARIE CURIE • LEAVES
THUNDER AND LIGHTNING

SEARCH LIGHT

These sentences are all mixed up. See if you can fix them.
Heat energy comes from the things people or animals eat.
Food energy comes from things that burn.

DID YOU KNOW?
Energy from food is measured in calories. A grownup needs to take in about 2,000-2,500 calories a day. Bicyclists in a major race eat three to five times that much, and they still sometimes run out of energy.

Answer: Heat energy comes from things that burn. Food energy comes from things people or animals eat.

SEARCH LIGHT

Find and correct the error in the following sentence: Leaves turn red if they have a lot of carbon dioxide in them when the sunlight shines on them.

The Science of Their Changing Colors

Trees that shed their leaves every year are called "deciduous" trees. Their leaves grow back again in spring.

Scientists think that plants get rid of things they can't use. After flowers have helped make new seeds for a plant, their petals fall off. And soon after leaves have lost their green stuff, called "chlorophyll," they fall off.

A leaf's chlorophyll uses sunlight to make sugar out of water and carbon dioxide, a gas in the air. Plants need carbon dioxide to live and grow. When leaves use carbon dioxide, another gas, called "oxygen," is left over. The plant can't use the oxygen. So it lets the oxygen go.

Animals and humans need oxygen to live. Their bodies use the oxygen, and what do you think they have left over? Carbon dioxide. When animals and humans breathe out, they let the carbon dioxide go.

It's easy to see that plants and animals and humans help each other this way.

In places where it gets cool in autumn, a plant loses its chlorophyll, and its leaves may turn yellow or red. The yellow was there all summer, but there was so much green that the yellow didn't show until the green went away.

Yellow leaves turn red only if they have lots of sugar in their sap and the sunlight shines on them. The more sugar a leaf has, the redder it becomes. If a leaf is kept in the shade, it will stay yellow even if it has a lot of sugar.

LEARN MORE! READ THESE ARTICLES…
LUTHER BURBANK • ENERGY • RAINBOWS

DID YOU KNOW?
Deciduous forests are one of the world's six major life zones: the often frozen tundra, the mostly evergreen taiga, temperate (mild) deciduous forest, tropical rainforest, grassland and savanna, and desert.

Answer: Leaves turn red if they have a lot of sugar in them when the sunlight shines on them.

SEARCH LIGHT

Temperature
measures how
much
a) heat something has.
b) chill something has.
c) pressure something has.

DID YOU KNOW?

If you test too-hot bath water with your foot, you're likely to burn that foot. That's because it takes longer for your foot to recognize temperature than it does your hand.

Hot and Cold

We can use our fingers, our tongue, or almost any part of our skin to feel just how hot or how cold something is. This is important because our bodies need just the right amount of heat so that we can live comfortably.

When it's cold and we want to make a room warmer, we turn on the heaters. In the summer when it's hot and we want to make the room cooler, do we add cold to the room?

No. We take away some of the heat. We say something is cold when it doesn't have much heat. The less heat it has, the colder it is.

Air conditioners suck hot air from a room. Pipes inside the air conditioners take a lot of heat out of the air, making it cold. Then a blower fans the cooled air into the room again.

When we want to know exactly how hot or how cold something is, we use a thermometer. A thermometer tells us about temperature—that is, how hot something is. Some countries measure temperature in "degrees Fahrenheit (° F)." Others use a different measuring system of "degrees Celsius (° C)."

We can use thermometers to measure air temperature, oven temperature, even body temperature. And your body temperature tells not only whether you feel hot or cold but whether you're healthy.

LEARN MORE! READ THESE ARTICLES…
DEW.• LIQUIDS, SOLIDS, AND GASES • VOLCANOES

Answer: a) heat something has.

DID YOU KNOW?

People used to think that tiny spider webs in the grass were actually the beds of fairies. This is because the webs, covered with dew, looked like magic nets.

Diamond Drops of Water

SEARCH LIGHT

How does warm air make dew?

Susan and her mother had come to the park for an early morning walk. The weather had been nice and warm recently. The nights were still, and there was hardly a cloud in the sky.

The park's grass glittered and winked. "Are those diamonds?" Susan asked. It looked as if someone had sprinkled tiny diamonds all across the grass during the night.

© W. Perry Conway/Corbis

Susan bent down to touch one of the glittering points. "It's water!" she cried out in surprise. "How did it get here? Did it rain last night?"

"No, this isn't rainwater. It's dew."

"What's dew?" Susan was eager to know.

"It came from the air. All air has some water in it, you know," said Mother.

"But I don't see any water in the air," said Susan, looking around.

"No, of course you don't. It's in the form of **vapor**, like fog, only very light," said Mother.

"So how does the water get onto the grass?"

"You know that steam turns into water again if it touches something cold, right?" Susan nodded. "Well, on certain nights the air is warm and full of moisture," Mother continued, "but the grass and the ground are cool. So when the vapor in the warm air touches these cooler surfaces..."

"...it changes to water drops on the grass," finished Susan. "That must be why sometimes in the morning our car is covered with tiny drops of water."

"That's right," Mother smiled. "Now let's get going on that walk!"

LEARN MORE! READ THESE ARTICLES...
CLOUDS • DIAMONDS • LIQUIDS, SOLIDS, AND GASES

Floating Water

Have you ever looked up at the clouds and wondered what they're made of?

Well, they're made of water—thousands of gallons of water, floating high in the air.

It's easier to believe this when you know that cloud water takes the form of tiny droplets. The droplets are so tiny that you couldn't see one if it was separated from all the others.

Sometimes the water droplets join together around tiny pieces of dust in the air. These drops get bigger and bigger as more droplets collect. When they become too heavy to float, they fall—"plop!" That's rain!

There are three main kinds of clouds. "Cumulus" refers to the small puffballs or great wooly-looking clouds that are flat on the bottom. "Stratus" are low clouds, usually streaky or without much shape. And "cirrus" are light feathery clouds, like the ones in the photo. Sometimes cirrus clouds are so high, where the air is very cold, that the whole cloud is made of ice.

Adding "nimbus" to any of these names changes it to mean a rain cloud. Tall white cottony rain clouds are called "cumulonimbus," or thunderheads. They often bring thunderstorms. Flat gray rain clouds are called "nimbostratus." They usually bring only rain.

Snow, **sleet**, and **hail** also fall from clouds. Snow and sleet fall only on cold winter days. Hailstones can fall even on a warm summer day.

And you may not realize it, but you've probably been right inside a cloud yourself. A cloud so close to the ground that we can walk through it is what we know as "fog."

LEARN MORE! READ THESE ARTICLES…
LIQUIDS, SOLIDS, AND GASES
RAINBOWS • THUNDER AND LIGHTNING

SEARCH LIGHT

Which of the following describes a cumulonimbus cloud?
a) cloud on the ground
b) sleet cloud
c) fog
d) thunderhead

DID YOU KNOW?

Being on "cloud nine" means you are feeling especially good, flying high. One explanation for the term comes from the military, where cloud types were numbered. Type nine was a tall thunder cloud, and jets would have to fly very high to get over one.

Arcs of Color

If you've ever looked at a rainbow and wondered how all those bright colors got in the sky, you're not alone.

The ancient Greeks thought these **arcs** of color were signs from the gods to warn people that terrible wars or storms were going to happen. The Norse people believed a rainbow was a bridge the gods used to walk down from the sky to the Earth. Other legends said there was a pot of gold waiting at the end of a rainbow.

But as beautiful as rainbows are, they aren't magic. And they aren't solid enough to walk on. In fact, a rainbow is just colored light. The seven colors are always the same and appear in the same order: red, orange, yellow, green, blue, indigo (a very deep blue), and violet. The name "Roy G. Biv" helps you remember the first letters and the order of the colors.

Rainbows often appear after or at the end of a storm—when the Sun is shining again but there is still some rain in the air. The sunlight looks white, but all seven rainbow colors are mixed together in it. So when a beam of sunlight passes through raindrops, it's broken into the seven different colors.

But you don't have to wait for rain to see rainbows. They can show up in the spray of a fountain or a waterfall, or you can make your own with a hose. Set the nozzle to create a spray, aim it away from the Sun, and then stand between the Sun and the spray. You've got an instant rainbow!

LEARN MORE! READ THESE ARTICLES…
CLOUDS · ECHOES · THUNDER AND LIGHTNING

SEARCH LIGHT

How can the name "Roy G. Biv" help you remember the colors of the rainbow?

DID YOU KNOW?

In spite of some legends, there really is no "end" of a rainbow. Rainbows are actually full circles. But because we can see only a limited distance, to the horizon of Earth and sky, we see only part of the circle.

Answer: The name gives you the first letter of each of the colors of the rainbow, in the order that they occur in the rainbow. Like this: Red Orange Yellow Green Blue Indigo Violet.

Nature's Fireworks

It can be fun playing in a gentle rain, splashing in puddles and chasing raindrops. But this would be a dangerous thing to do when there are thunderheads above.

Thunderheads are the large, dark, often fast-moving clouds that come out during storms. Thunderheads rumble mightily during storms, and that rumbling indicates the presence of lightning. The rumbling is the sound lightning makes as it arcs across the sky.

During a thunderstorm, electricity collects in the clouds. And often that electricity gets released as lightning. It's dangerous to be out when lightning is a possibility because lightning can quite easily kill from miles away. People have died from lightning strikes even though the storm the lightning came from was barely visible on the **horizon**.

Lightning bolts frequently race to the ground, drawn by objects such as trees and lamp posts that are especially good conductors of electricity. Lightning is most attracted to tall objects, which is why trees, buildings, and radio towers are often struck.

Actually, there are two parts to a lightning strike. The bolt from the sky is the part we don't see, because it is so fast and faint. The part we do see is the return strike. This is a bright flash of lightning that jumps up out of the ground to meet the lightning coming down and then races up to the base of the clouds.

Lightning can hurt or kill people who are struck by it. If you ever are caught in a lightning storm, get inside quickly. Or get into a car. Lightning that hits a car will travel into the ground harmlessly.

LEARN MORE! READ THESE ARTICLES...
CLOUDS • ECHOES • RAINBOWS

SEARCH LIGHT

True or false?
In a thunderstorm it's a good idea to take shelter under a tree.

DID YOU KNOW?
Florida is known as the "lightning capital of the world." Every year lightning strikes in Florida more often than any other state in the United States. Also, lightning kills more people in Florida than in any other state.

© A & J Verkaik/Corbis

Answer: FALSE. A tree is likely to be struck by lightning in a storm. It's better to get inside a car or a house, which will protect you even if it's struck.

SEARCH LIGHT

Fill in
the blank:
The quietest
part of a cyclone
is the _____,
where there are
no winds or clouds.

Nature's Fury

A cyclone is a **rotating** storm that can be hundreds of miles across. These storms can be very destructive. The winds in a cyclone usually blow at more than 75 miles per hour.

When a cyclone starts in the warmer waters of the Atlantic Ocean, it is called a "hurricane." In the western Pacific Ocean, it is known as a "typhoon."

From above, a cyclone looks like a huge spinning doughnut of clouds. The center of the storm, the doughnut hole, is called the "eye." The eye is quiet and cloudless. When the eye passes overhead, it might seem like the storm has ended. But within an hour or two, the eye passes and the other side of the storm hits.

With its strong winds a cyclone also brings flooding rains and sometimes very high ocean waves. When a cyclone hits land, it causes severe damage. The combination of wind, rain, and waves can knock down trees, flatten houses, and wash away roads.

Most cyclones start over **tropical** oceans because areas of warm water are their source of energy. Strong rotating winds that start on land are called a "tornado." A tornado, such as the one pictured here, starts for different reasons and is smaller than a cyclone. But a tornado also has very strong winds, so it too can be very destructive. It can knock a train off its track or lift a house straight into the air. Fortunately, tornadoes usually die soon after they start.

LEARN MORE! READ THESE ARTICLES…
CLOUDS • TSUNAMIS • WAVES

Paul and LindaMarie Ambrose/Taxi/Getty Images

DID YOU KNOW?
The best way for scientists to learn a cyclone's size and strength is to fly a plane through it. That's the most sure way—but certainly not the safest!

Answer: The quietest part of a cyclone is the eye, where there are no winds or clouds.

Killer Downpour

Rain seems to make things cleaner, doesn't it? Rain helps flowers grow and helps keep plants green. It washes the dust from cars and houses. It leaves roads shiny. And it leaves a fresh smell in the air.

Scientist testing polluted lake water containing melted acid snow.
© Ted Spiegel/Corbis

But rain can be dirty. That's because as the rain falls, it gathers up any **pollution** that's in the air. It can leave cars looking streaky and windows spotty.

Some rain will even ruin the paint on cars. It will damage or kill the plants it falls on and the fish living in lakes that are fed by rain. Such rain is called "acid rain."

This is how it happens. We burn fuels such as coal, gas, and oil in our factories. This releases gases containing **elements** such as sulfur, carbon, and nitrogen into the air. These combine with moisture in the air to form damaging substances such as sulfuric acid, carbonic acid, and nitric acid. When it rains, these acids fall to earth with the water.

Acid doesn't fall to earth only in the form of rain. It can also fall as snow, sleet, and hail. It can even be in fog.

Acid rain harms many forms of life, including human life. It also damages buildings. The acid eats through stone, metal, and concrete. Acid rain has injured some of the world's great monuments, including the **cathedrals** of Europe, the Colosseum in Rome, and the Taj Mahal in India.

LEARN MORE! READ THESE ARTICLES...
CLOUDS • LEAVES • LIQUIDS, SOLIDS, AND GASES

SEARCH LIGHT

Acid rain can cause
a) water to become polluted.
b) fish to die.
c) the outside of buildings to wear down.
d) plants to die.
e) all of the above.

The unhealthy branch on the left shows the damage
that acid rain can do to plants.
© Ted Spiegel/Corbis

DID YOU KNOW?
Acid rain destroys trees. We need
trees to make oxygen and to get rid
of carbon dioxide, which can be
poisonous to us. Just one acre of
trees gets rid of 2.5 tons of carbon
dioxide a year.

Answer: e) all of the above.

DID YOU KNOW?
According to researchers in Canada, the tallest ocean wave ever recorded was 112 feet high.

Movement on the Seas

The ocean never seems to sit still. Its waves rise and fall. On beaches they push forward and fall back. But what makes ocean water into waves?

Most waves are created by the wind. The wind blows along the surface of the water and forces waves in the same direction. The top of a wave is called the "crest," and the lowest part in between the crests is known as the "trough." When waves roll through the open ocean, they're called "swell." As they reach the shore, their crests get higher and closer together and finally topple over. Then they're called "breakers" or "surf."

A gentle wind makes long waves that don't rise very high. But stronger winds push harder on the water and create taller waves. Big storms mean strong winds, and that means huge, powerful waves.

Major ocean storms, called "hurricanes" or "typhoons," can cause enormous waves. Some are so big they can smash oceanside houses into pieces or tip over ships that get in their way. During violent storms waves have been known to reach to the tops of lighthouses and to toss boats completely out of the water.

The most destructive waves are tsunamis, but they're quite different from other waves. Tsunamis—also wrongly called "tidal waves"—are not caused by tides or by the wind. These huge waves are created by underwater earthquakes or volcanic eruptions.

SEARCH LIGHT

"Breakers" is another word for
a) surf.
b) trough.
c) crest.

LEARN MORE! READ THESE ARTICLES...
CYCLONES AND TORNADOES • SAND • TSUNAMIS

Without waves the very popular sport of surfing wouldn't be possible. Riding a surfboard in waves like these requires great balance, skill, and a lot of nerve!
© Rick Doyle/Corbis

Answer: a) surf.

Waves of Destruction

A powerful earthquake struck the coast of Chile in 1960. Frightened, people got into their boats and went to the harbor to escape the disaster. Soon enormous waves caused by the earthquake rose up from the ocean. These violent waves, each more than three stories high, destroyed all the boats and killed the people in them. The waves then traveled for 15 hours across the Pacific Ocean to Hilo in Hawaii, where they destroyed more property.

These waves are known as "tsunamis," from the Japanese for "harbor wave."

A tsunami is a large destructive wave created by the shock from an earthquake or volcanic eruption. The impact of a **meteorite** could also create a tsunami. Tsunamis travel fast and have the force to destroy entire coastal communities within moments.

A tsunami can travel at speeds of 450 miles per hour or more (as fast as a jet plane) and packs tremendous force. As the tsunami approaches land, it grows larger. It continues to travel until its energy is completely used up. All low-lying coastal areas are **vulnerable** to a tsunami disaster.

In July 1998 a tsunami **devastated** the northwest coast of Papua New Guinea. It was caused by an earthquake 12 miles offshore that measured 7.0 on the Richter scale. (The biggest earthquakes have not reached higher than 9.0.) The tsunami swept away three coastal villages. Nothing remained afterward but sand.

SEARCH LIGHT

Which of these does *not* cause a tsunami?
a) earthquake
b) volcanic eruption
c) high winds

LEARN MORE! READ THESE ARTICLES...
CYCLONES AND TORNADOES • VOLCANOES • WAVES

DID YOU KNOW?
When tsunamis strike land, they generally first suck all the water out of any harbors.

Answer: c) high winds

To most of us, this landscape is beautiful. But to a geologist, it also tells the story of millions of years of Earth's history.

© Layne Kennedy/Corbis

Studying the Earth

How did the Earth get its shape?

What was the world like millions of years ago?

What is the Earth made of?

Why do earthquakes happen?

These are some of the many questions that geologists try to answer. Geologists are people who study the Earth's form and its history. The word "geology" comes from Greek words meaning "earth science."

Geology is an important science. Geologists help others to find useful fossil fuels such as oil and coal that lie hidden in the Earth's crust. Geologists also help figure out where earthquakes are likely to happen. This helps people know where it's safest to put up buildings.

Because there are so many things about the Earth that geologists study, geology is divided into many individual areas. For instance, the study of physical geology looks at the changes that take place inside the Earth and the reasons for those changes. Geochemistry is concerned with the chemical **elements** that make up rocks, soil, and **minerals**. Petrology deals with rocks themselves.

Did you know that paleontology is a form of geology? Paleontologists study life forms that existed on Earth millions of years ago, from the tiniest **bacteria** to the most enormous dinosaurs. But because these creatures died so many millions of years ago, their bodies have turned into fossils—living things preserved as rock.

LEARN MORE! READ THESE ARTICLES...
DINOSAURS: A MYSTERY DISAPPEARANCE
FOSSILS • ROCKS AND MINERALS

SEARCH LIGHT

Match the scientist with what she studies:

geologist	Earth
petrologist	fossils
geochemist	rocks
paleontologist	chemicals in rocks

The Earth's Building Blocks

You might think that rocks are pretty dull. But rocks tell the history of the Earth, including stories of giant explosions, mountains rising from the sea, and buried forests turning to stone.

Most rocks are combinations of one or more **minerals**. Minerals are inorganic, which means they are not alive. Yet they are extremely important to all living things. Some minerals are metals, such as iron and gold. Other are nonmetallic, like quartz and calcite.

Some rocks contain the hardened **remains** of animals and plants. Limestone rock is usually made up largely of bits and pieces of fossil shells and skeletons of sea creatures.

Sandstone canyon.
© Scott T. Smith/Corbis

All rocks fall into one of three groups, depending on how they're created.

Igneous rocks are formed from cooling magma, which is the lava released in a volcanic eruption. The earliest rocks on Earth were igneous.

But rocks don't stay the same forever. They break down into small pieces because of wind, water, and ice. And when small pieces of rock settle together, they're known as "sediment." As layers settle on other layers over many years, their weight squeezes the pieces together into solid sedimentary rock. Both photos show the very common sedimentary rock called "sandstone," which is cemented sand.

The third group of rocks gets its name from the word "metamorphosis," which means "change." Metamorphic rocks are created when extreme temperatures or pressures cause changes in igneous or sedimentary rocks. Marble is a metamorphic rock formed from intensely squeezed and heated limestone. And limestone, you'll remember, began as seashells and skeletons. It's another amazing Earth story told by a rock!

LEARN MORE! READ THESE ARTICLES...
CHALK • SAND • VOLCANOES

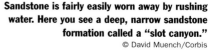

Sandstone is fairly easily worn away by rushing water. Here you see a deep, narrow sandstone formation called a "slot canyon."
© David Muench/Corbis

SEARCH LIGHT

Minerals are inorganic, which means they are not _____.

Answer: Minerals are inorganic, which means they are not alive.

DID YOU KNOW?
Much of the chalk on Earth dates from 66 million to 144 million years ago. So much chalk comes from this time, in fact, that the whole period was named the Cretaceous Period, from the Latin word for "chalk."

The Remains
of Tiny Shells

SEARCH LIGHT

Why does it take millions of years to make chalk?

The material we call "chalk" had its beginnings during the time when dinosaurs lived on Earth. At that time the oceans were rising higher and higher until finally they covered most of the Earth's land.

In those oceans lived billions of tiny animals. They were so small you could not have seen them—even smaller than the period at the end of this sentence. These tiny creatures had shells made of the **element** calcium. When these animals died, their shells fell to the bottom of the oceans. After thousands of years there were many layers of shells on the ocean floor.

As more and more of the tiny shells pressed down from the top, those on the bottom became harder and began to stick together. Eventually the shells changed into a **mineral** called "calcite," the main ingredient of the rock known as "limestone."

Drawing chalk, an entirely different material from natural chalk.
© Michael T. Sedam/Corbis

Many millions of years passed after the first chalk was made. The Earth's surface changed its shape, and the land and sea developed new shorelines. This left many chalk layers on dry land, both in the middle of **continents** and along coastlines. In some parts of England there are chalk cliffs 800 feet high. These are the famous White Cliffs of Dover, and they are almost solid chalk!

If you had a piece of chalk from those cliffs, you could use it to write on a chalkboard. But the chalk that you now use in classrooms is not a piece dug from the cliffs or the ground. It is made in factories by mixing several other materials together.

LEARN MORE! READ THESE ARTICLES . . .
FOSSILS • GEOLOGY • ROCKS AND MINERALS

The fabulous White Cliffs of Dover in England
are made of chalk millions of years old.
© Bob Krist/Corbis

Answer: Many shells have to pile up to be heavy enough to press the bottom ones together and change them into stone.

39

The Nitty-Gritty

You can find sand at the edge of lakes, the bottoms of rivers, and the seashore. You can find it in mountain valleys, deserts, and, of course, a sandbox. Where does all this sand come from?

Sand is created when rocks break into tiny, tiny pieces. Wind, ice, and rain knock against high mountain cliffs. And slowly, over millions of years, these forces break off pieces of rock. The pieces bounce down the mountainside and break off other pieces of rock—while it's also breaking into smaller and smaller pieces itself. It isn't sand yet, but it's getting there.

Rivers and glaciers are also good at making sand. A river's water rushes along, carrying rocks with it and breaking them into little pieces. The ice of a glacier grinds away at whatever rocks it slowly rolls across.

Another great sand maker is the ocean. Every day, all over the world, tides rise and fall, pushing against rocks over and over. Waves tear at the rocks along the shore, wearing them down.

Thanks to the weather, water, and ice, some of these broken rocks finally get so small that they become what we call "sand."

Now that you have all this sand, what can you do with it? Sand is used for paving roads. Bricks made with sand are harder and stronger than other bricks. Sand is also used to filter (or clean) water. When it's sprayed with great force against stone or brick, it can grind away thick layers of dirt or even paint in a process called "sandblasting."

And, of course, sand is great for building sand castles!

LEARN MORE! READ THESE ARTICLES…
ATOMS · ROCKS AND MINERALS · WAVES

Mounds or ridges of sand like these are called "sand dunes." They're caused by the combined action of wind and gravity.
© Dave G. Houser/Corbis

SEARCH LIGHT

True or false? Sand can be used to clean buildings.

DID YOU KNOW?

Once a year the Harrison Hot Springs resort in British Columbia, Canada, holds the world championship of sand sculpting. The rules say sculptures can be made only of water and sand, and they must be finished in under 100 work hours.

Answer: TRUE. Sandblasting is a powerful process for cleaning stone or brick.

41

The Hardest-Working Gemstones in the World

Diamonds were made millions and millions of years ago when fuming volcanoes melted the **element** called "carbon" inside some rocks. Gigantic masses of earth pressed the carbon tightly. The hot melted carbon was squeezed so tightly that by the time it cooled, it had changed into the hard **gemstones** called "diamonds."

Diamond jewelry.
© Lynn Goldsmith/Corbis

Some diamonds are found in the gravel and sand near rivers. Others are left in the mountains by **glaciers**. Most diamonds are mined from rocks deep underground, usually in Africa. The country of South Africa is the major source for the diamonds used in jewelry.

Diamonds usually look like pieces of glass or dull stones when they're first taken out of the ground. They must be cut and shaped to be used in jewelry. And diamonds are so hard that nothing can cut them except another diamond.

Using diamond-edged tools, the diamond cutter carefully shapes and polishes the diamond so that it has straight edges and smooth surfaces. These edges and surfaces help the diamond reflect light so that it sparkles and flashes with tiny bursts of color.

Diamonds often seem to flash like white fire. But there are diamonds that have other colors. Red, blue, and green diamonds are difficult to find. Yellow, orange, and violet diamonds are more common. Sometimes people even find black diamonds.

Only the clearest diamonds become glittering gems. But because of their hardness, even dull-looking diamonds are still valuable as cutting tools. These are called "**industrial** diamonds." Only about 25 percent of all diamonds are fine enough to become jewels, so most of the world's diamonds are the hard-working industrial type.

LEARN MORE! READ THESE ARTICLES...
DEW • GEOLOGY • ROCKS AND MINERALS

SEARCH LIGHT

Fill in the blank: Diamonds are so hard that only
_____
can cut them.

DID YOU KNOW?

The Hope diamond is one of the biggest blue diamonds known in the world. Unfortunately, it is supposed to be cursed. Several of its owners have died tragically or have had very bad luck.

Raw diamonds look like chunks of glass when they're first found.
© Dave G. Houser/Corbis

Answer: Diamonds are so hard that only another diamond can cut them.

DID YOU KNOW?
The remains of ancient Pompeii and the other cities buried by Mount Vesuvius' eruption were amazingly preserved. Loaves of bread that had been baking at the moment were found. These discoveries marked the beginning of the modern science of archaeology.

Mountains of Smoke and Fire

Deep under the Earth's surface it's so hot that even rock melts. Sometimes this molten rock, called "magma," is pushed up to the Earth's surface. At that point it is referred to as "lava." And the opening, or vent, that lets the lava out is a volcano.

A volcano may explode violently, throwing rocks for miles. Or it might push the lava out so that it flows away, cools, and hardens. Some volcanoes release clouds of poisonous gas or huge clouds of ash. Volcanoes can even do all these things underwater.

Most volcanoes have been around for a very long time. Many haven't erupted in years and have cooled off. Volcanoes that won't be erupting anymore are called "dead volcanoes."

Some volcanoes still let off smoke. These "sleeping volcanoes" may "wake up" someday and start erupting. Mount Vesuvius in Italy slept for a thousand years. But one day in AD 79 it suddenly woke up. Its eruption spewed hot ash and rocky fragments that buried the city of Pompeii. A hot mud flow buried nearby Herculaneum. The remains are so well preserved that the area has been named a World Heritage site.

But not all volcanoes are destructive. If a volcano spits out enough lava and **debris**, it piles up into a mountain. The Hawaiian Islands and the island of Iceland were created this way.

Other volcanoes help provide heat and energy. Many Icelandic homes get their hot water from springs heated by volcanic steam. That steam can also be used to produce electricity. Also, plants grow very well in the rich soil left by volcanoes. And valuable gems, such as diamonds, can sometimes be found in the rocks that volcanoes spit out.

SEARCH LIGHT

Which of the following is *not* often spit out by volcanoes?

a) lava   d) ash
b) oil   e) steam
c) gas

LEARN MORE! READ THESE ARTICLES...
LIQUIDS, SOLIDS, AND GASES • ROCKS AND MINERALS • TSUNAMIS

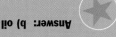

Ancient Life in Stone

Would you like to see something that lived millions of years ago? You can if you find a fossil.

The **remains** or traces of plants, animals, and even **bacteria** that are preserved in stone are called "fossils." If you've ever pressed a coin into clay and then removed it, you've seen the sort of image you'll find in many fossils. The original thing isn't there anymore, but there's an **impression** of it left in the stone.

Fossilized fern.
© Wolfgang Kaehler/Corbis

Many fossils are easy to recognize as the living things they once were. The plant fossil you see in the smaller photo here, for example, looks like the tracing of a fern leaf.

Usually, the harder portions of an **organism** are what last long enough to become fossils. Sometimes the hard structures are preserved almost whole. For instance, entire fossilized dinosaur bones have been petrified, or changed to a stony substance.

Fossils are not always easy to find. Only a small fraction of all ancient life ever became fossils. And the fossils that did form are often buried deep underground.

You can tell the fossils in the big photo used to be fish. After they died—millions of years ago—they sank to the riverbed and became covered with soft mud. Their flesh wasted away, but their bones were held together by the mud.

Eventually, the river dried up. It was filled with dust and dirt blown by the winds. The bones of the fish stayed where they were. Slowly, the mud of the riverbed turned to stone.

Finally, somebody found this fossil while digging where the river once was.

LEARN MORE! READ THESE ARTICLES…
CHARLES DARWIN
DINOSAURS: GIANTS OF THE PAST
MAMMOTHS AND MASTODONS

SEARCH LIGHT

It's unusual to see an animal fossil that shows more than just the bones. Why do you think bones are usually the best-preserved parts?

This fossil shows a rare picture of life in action millions of years ago. Look carefully, and you can see that a big fish was eating a smaller one when they both died.
© Layne Kennedy/Corbis

DID YOU KNOW?

Over millions of years, many plant and animal remains have turned into the coal, oil, and natural gas we use for fuel. These underground energy sources are known as "fossil fuels."

Answer: It takes a long time for a fossil to form. Bones last much longer than flesh and organs do. So only the bones were left by the time the fish turned into a fossil.

Giants of the Past

The word "dinosaur" means "terrible lizard." It is a name given to lizard-like animals that lived long, long ago. Many of the dinosaurs were the largest and scariest creatures that ever walked on land. All of them, large and small, were part of the animal group known as "reptiles." The dinosaurs were the ancient cousins of today's crocodiles, snakes, and lizards.

You may be familiar with the brontosaur, or "thunder lizard." What you may not know is that this dinosaur is now called apatosaur, meaning "dishonest lizard." A mix-up in **fossil** bones gave scientists the wrong idea of what it looked like. The apatosaur was still pretty impressive, as much as 70 feet long. No matter what you call it, this creature certainly must have sounded like thunder when it walked.

There were many different kinds of dinosaurs:

The tyrannosaur (*Tyrannosaurus rex*) was the "king of the lizards" and was as long as a fire truck. For many years the tyrannosaur was thought to be the largest carnivore, or meat-eating animal, ever to have lived on Earth. But the giganotosaur was an even larger carnivore!

The anatosaur is called the "duck lizard" because it had a bill like a duck—though there were 2,000 un-duck-like teeth in its cheeks!

The triceratops was the "three-horned lizard." Many of these dinosaurs once lived in the western United States.

There were many other kinds of dinosaurs—more than 1,000 different **species**. And they once lived almost everywhere in the world.

LEARN MORE! READ THESE ARTICLES...
DINOSAURS: A MYSTERY DISAPPEARANCE
FOSSILS · TYRANNOSAUR

DID YOU KNOW?
If you hold up your hand, you'll be looking at something still smaller than a tyrannosaur tooth.

SEARCH LIGHT

Find and correct the error in the following sentence: The apatosaur's name means "dishonest lizard," referring to the beast's habit of robbing its neighbors.

Answer: The apatosaur's name means "dishonest lizard," referring to the mix-up in fossils that confused scientists.

DID YOU KNOW?

Scientists think that some dinosaurs swallowed rocks, just as some birds do, to help break up food in their bellies.

A Mystery
Disappearance

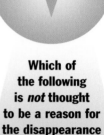

Many of the dinosaurs that once roamed the Earth were so big and strong that they didn't need to be afraid of any living thing. So why aren't there dinosaurs today?

Some scientists think that when new kinds of plants began to grow on Earth, dinosaurs couldn't eat them. New kinds of animals smaller than dinosaurs also appeared during this time. They may have been able to survive better than the dinosaurs. It's also possible that disease killed dinosaurs by the millions.

Not all scientists think that all dinosaurs died at once. Another explanation is that a changing **climate** killed them. We know that when they were living, the weather began to change. Summers grew shorter and winters grew colder. In some places heat waves dried up rivers and swamps. Elsewhere, new lakes and rivers appeared, and many places were flooded. Some dinosaurs may have died because it gradually became too cold or too hot for them.

Many scientists believe that dinosaurs died because an **asteroid** struck the Earth about 65 million years ago. The dust raised by the impact would have blocked out sunlight for months, so that plants stopped growing and the temperature dropped. When plant-eating dinosaurs died from lack of food, so would the meat eaters that hunted them.

Some scientists think that many dinosaurs **evolved** into birds. So the next time you see a robin, consider that you may be looking at a dinosaur's relative.

Which of the following is *not* thought to be a reason for the disappearance of dinosaurs?
a) an asteroid striking Earth
b) climate change
c) disease
d) poisoned plants
e) flood

LEARN MORE! READ THESE ARTICLES…
DINOSAURS: GIANTS OF THE PAST • FOSSILS
MAMMOTHS AND MASTODONS

Dinosaur tracks remain, but scientists still don't know what happened to the giant creatures that made them.
© Tom Bean/Corbis

The Tyrant King

It was longer than a bus, weighed more than four tons, and had teeth up to a foot long. The tyrannosaur may have died out 65 million years ago, but it is still one of the largest meat-eating land animals that ever lived. It's no wonder that the first scientist who discovered this frightening creature's bones called it *Tyrannosaurus rex*: "**tyrant** lizard king."

Dinosaurs were not true lizards. When scientists first discovered tyrannosaur **fossils**, however, they did believe that such a dangerous-looking animal would have been a powerful and mean bully among the dinosaurs. The tyrannosaur's jagged teeth and huge jaws make it clear that the tyrannosaur was a powerful carnivore, or meat eater.

Tyrannosaurs lived mainly in what is now North America and Asia. The creature was about 40 feet long from its head to its thick and heavy tail. The tyrannosaur probably stooped forward, with the big tail balancing its weight when it walked.

The tyrannosaur had large, powerful rear legs but small front arms. These forearms wouldn't even have been able to reach its mouth. So the tyrannosaur probably planted its clawed rear feet on a dead animal, bit hard, and ripped the flesh away from the **carcass**.

The tyrannosaur is one of the most popular of all dinosaurs, thanks to movies and books. But scientists still don't know a lot about the beast. Did it hunt by sight or by smell? Was tyrannosaur a hunter at all, or did it just eat dead animals it found? Was it a fast runner?

With so many questions, we're still getting to know the tyrannosaur—but from a safe distance!

LEARN MORE! READ THESE ARTICLES...
DINOSAURS: GIANTS OF THE PAST • ENERGY • FOSSILS

SEARCH LIGHT

Find and correct the error in the following sentence: *Tyrannosaurus rex* means "tyrant wizard king."

DID YOU KNOW?

Tyrannosaur fossils show features that support the theory that dinosaurs may be the distant ancestors of birds. For instance, its bones were very lightweight for their size, just as birds' are. And its walking posture resembles that of modern birds.

Sue, the famous *T. rex* in Chicago's Field Museum, was sick when she was alive. Researchers say that she suffered from gout, a painful disease that causes swelling in bones and joints.
Courtesy, Field Museum

SEARCH LIGHT

Mammoths
and mastodons
are related to
a) horses.
b) elephants.
c) dinosaurs.

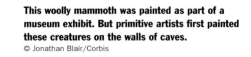

This woolly mammoth was painted as part of a
museum exhibit. But primitive artists first painted
these creatures on the walls of caves.
© Jonathan Blair/Corbis

Ancient Elephants

Believe it or not, thousands of years ago some elephants wore heavy fur coats.

Actually, the mammoth was an ancestor of the modern elephant. And mastodons were distant relatives of the mammoth. Neither animal is around today. But at one time they roamed the Earth in great numbers.

We know a lot about these ancient creatures because scientists have found many frozen mammoth bodies, especially in the icy area of Russia known as Siberia. Both beasts largely died out at the end of the last Ice Age, about 10,000 years ago. The mammoth didn't show up until about 1 1/2 million years ago.

Mastodons and mammoths were a lot alike, but the mastodons were on the planet first. They appeared about 20 million years ago. They were smaller than mammoths and had thick legs like pillars. Mastodons were covered with long reddish brown hair.

Mammoths were the size of modern elephants. The woolly mammoth had a thick furry yellowish brown undercoat with longer bristly hair over it. Like the mastodon, the mammoth had small ears and very long tusks. Despite these dangerous tusks, both animals ate only grass and other plants. The tusks may have been for shoveling snow and ice to uncover food.

Mastodons and mammoths were around at the same time as early humans. The people of the day hunted the animals, but hunting didn't wipe them out. Scientists think that the mastodon and the mammoth vanished because the **glaciers** of the Ice Age destroyed much of the vegetation they relied on for food.

LEARN MORE! READ THESE ARTICLES...
DINOSAURS: A MYSTERY DISAPPEARANCE
FOSSILS • GEOLOGY

DID YOU KNOW?
In 1816, when coal-gas lights were first being used, one of the first museum exhibits to be lit with the new invention was a mastodon skeleton.

Answer: b) elephants.

Inventing New Plants

Luther Burbank grew up on a farm in the United States. Though he had only a high school education, he had read Charles Darwin's ideas about how living things change over time. Burbank wanted to understand why different plants had their own kind of fruit and flowers—and how they might be changed to grow better ones.

In the 1870s most people didn't think it was possible to make new kinds of plants. But Burbank surprised them by creating hundreds of new varieties, including a white blackberry so clear that you could see its seeds through its skin. Burbank grew a tomato on a potato vine and called it a "pomato." He combined a plum tree and an apricot tree to make a new fruit called a "plumcot."

Benefiting today from Burbank's work with plants.
© Lynda Richardson/Corbis

Burbank produced many of these plants by "grafting." He took a small twig from one plant and put it into a cut he had made on a different plant. The plant with roots controlled the size of the new plant, while the twig grew into branches with flowers and fruit. Sometimes he produced completely new kinds of plants by cross-pollination. He did this by putting **pollen** from the flowers of one type of plant onto the sticky part of the flowers of another type of plant.

Getting the new plants he wanted was not easy. The white blackberry took Burbank 65,000 tries to get right. And he spent eight years cross-pollinating different types of daisy to turn a small yellowish daisy into a tall snow-white flower with a yellow center. The result was the famous Shasta daisy.

Burbank's work produced many useful plants. And his experiments added greatly to the knowledge of how features pass from parents to offspring.

LEARN MORE! READ THESE ARTICLES...
CHARLES DARWIN • FOSSILS • LEAVES

SEARCH LIGHT

Find and correct the error in the following sentence: Rafting is a way of making new plants by sticking a twig of one plant into a cut on another plant.

Answer: Grafting is a way of making new plants by sticking a twig of one plant into a cut on another plant.

DID YOU KNOW?
Not only did Marie Curie win the Nobel Prize twice, but her daughter and son-in-law, Irène and Frédéric Joliot-Curie, shared the Nobel Prize in 1935.

Discovering a New Kind of Science

The French scientist Marie Curie became the first woman to win the Nobel Prize, one of the greatest honors in the world. What's more, she was the first person ever to win the prize two times.

Marie, who was born in Poland, studied science at the Sorbonne, the great French university. She was one of the best students there. She worked very hard, often late into the night, sometimes eating little more than bread, butter, and tea day after day.

Marie married Pierre Curie after completing her science course. Pierre was also a scientist, and the two worked together. Another scientist, named Henri Becquerel, had already discovered that certain types of material send out tiny "bullets" of energy all the time. Marie called this action "radioactivity."

These strange radioactive **particles** were far too small to be seen, but it was possible to take a kind of photograph of them. Marie studied radioactivity and discovered two new elements that were radioactive, polonium and radium.

Over the years Marie Curie's discoveries about radioactivity have proved extremely important in many ways. Radioactivity helps doctors identify and treat diseases. A major form of power generation based on nuclear energy has been developed, a process involving radioactivity. And in geology, radioactivity is used to determine the age of ancient rocks.

Marie's entire life was spent working for science. She fell ill and eventually died because of working so closely with radioactive materials. She knew about this risk, but she felt her work was too important to stop. Marie Curie was awarded the Nobel Prize in 1903 for her work on radioactivity and in 1911 for discovering radium.

LEARN MORE! READ THESE ARTICLES…
ATOMS • ENERGY • GEOLOGY

SEARCH LIGHT

True or false? Marie Curie's research led to her death.

The Theory of Evolution

All cultures tell a story about how life came to be on Earth. Most traditions and religions tell of creation happening in a particular event. But what does science tell us? A scientist named Charles Darwin came up with a very different idea about how humans and other creatures came to be.

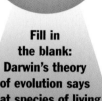

Fill in the blank: Darwin's theory of evolution says that species of living things _____ over time.

Darwin and his ideas being made fun of in a magazine.
© Archivo Iconographic/Corbis

In 1831, at age 22, Darwin set out from England on a scientific expedition aboard a ship called the *Beagle*. He sailed to the coast of South America and to some Pacific islands, such as the Galapagos.

On the trip, Darwin studied many **species**, or groups, of plants and animals. He also studied fossils—rocks that carry imprints of ancient plants and animals. The fossils showed that plants and animals living on Earth long ago were different from the same types of plants and animals that lived in his own time. Darwin wondered why these old species had disappeared and the new species had developed.

After much thought, here's what Darwin decided: Living things must work hard for food and shelter, so only those that do this best will survive. Small individual strengths, such as being bigger or faster, can be the keys to survival. And these strengths are passed on to the individuals' offspring. Helpful individual differences add up over time to make the whole species change, or evolve.

This was Darwin's famous **theory** of **evolution**. He also believed that over time the same species living in different surroundings could evolve into two separate species.

Darwin published his theory in his books *On the Origin of Species* and *The Descent of Man*. He proposed that all living things, including humans, have slowly evolved from earlier species. Many people do not accept Darwin's theory. But it remains the most widely accepted scientific theory.

LEARN MORE! READ THESE ARTICLES...
DINOSAURS: GIANTS OF THE PAST • FOSSILS • GEOLOGY

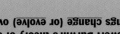
Answer: Darwin's theory of evolution says that species of living things change (or evolve) over time.

G L O S S A R Y

absorb soak up

arc a curved line

asteroid small, often rocklike heavenly body orbiting the Sun

bacterium (plural: bacteria) tiny one-celled organism too small to see with the unaided eye

carcass dead body or leftover parts of an animal

cathedral large church where a bishop is in charge

chemical one of the combined substances making up living and nonliving things

climate average weather in a particular area

continent one of the largest of Earth's landmasses

core central part

debris trash or fragments

devastate wreck or destroy

element in science, one of the simplest substances that make up all matter

evolve (noun: evolution) change, especially over time

fossil an imprint or other trace in rock of an animal, plant, or other living thing

gemstone natural material that can be cut and polished for use in jewelry

generate create or produce

glacier a large riverlike body of ice moving slowly down a slope or spreading over a land surface

hail small balls or lumps of ice that fall from the sky, as rain does

horizon distant point where the land and the sky appear to meet

impression mark or figure made by pressing one object onto the surface of another; also, the effect or feeling an object or person creates

indivisible unable to be divided

industrial having to do with businesses that construct or produce something

meteorite a mass of material from space that reaches the Earth's surface

mineral substance that is not animal or plant and is an important nutrient for living things

organism living thing

particle tiny bit or piece

pollen tiny, dusty reproductive parts of plants

pollute (noun: pollution) to poison or make dirty, often with man-made waste

potential possible

remains parts that are left after time passes or some event occurs

rotate spin or turn

sleet frozen or partly frozen rain

species a particular group of living things that share certain inherited features

theory in science, an idea or reasoned explanation for why things are as they are or why things happen as they do

tropical having to do with the Earth's warmest and most humid (moist) climates

tyrant powerful and cruel ruler; also, someone who acts like a tyrant

vapor a substance in the state of a gas (rather than a solid or liquid)

vulnerable exposed or in danger